The Bicycle Slow Race

Claire Bateman

WESLEYAN NEW POETS

The Bicycle Slow Race

Wesleyan University Press

Published by University Press of New England
Hanover and London

Wesleyan University Press
Published by University Press of New England
Hanover, New Hampshire 03755
© 1991 by Claire Bateman
All rights reserved
Printed in the United States of America
5 4 3 2 1
CIP data appear at the end of the book

Some of the poems in this collection previously
appeared in *Kenyon Review*, *Kenyon Poets Anthology*,
Louisiana Literature, *New Virginia Review*, *Plains
Poetry Journal*, *Poem*, *South Carolina Review*,
Southern Poetry Review, some in different form.
"Greek Myths" appeared in *The Chester A. Jones
Foundation National Poetry Competition Winners
1990*.

The author would like to thank Margaret Gibson for
her valuable help with several versions of the
manuscript.

Contents

The Bicycle Slow Race   1

Retroactive Causation   2

Becoming   3

Greek Myths   4

Berries   5

Refuge   6

The Frog Princess   7

If Worst Came to Worst   8

Vampire Tale   10

Pyrite   11

Flash Bulletin   12

Jamestown: Anne Burras   13

Trying   14

Pocahontas' Crossing   17

In the Icicle Garden   18

Initiation   19

Molting   21

Morning Tactics   22

Salvation   23

Map   24

Gloucester Women   25

Slugs   27

Reliable   29

Gravity   30

What Gifts They Have for Us   33

Hunger   34

Psyche and Her Sisters   35

Telling the Truth   36

Marvels   37

Claims Adjustment   38

The Nursery-Web Spider   39

Cost   41

Explicit   42

Loss of Advantage   43

Fifth Brandenburg   44

All Souls   45

That   47

To My Son, Who Is Afraid of Bugs   48

Technology   49

Not Thinking about God   50

The Gift: 1578   52

Properties of Salt   54

Shrinking   55

Resolution   57

Distances   58

The Bicycle Slow Race

The Bicycle Slow Race

Often I've seen friends brake when I drive the car,
the cables of their minds tightening
as they jam the spectral pedal
all the way down to the carpeted floor.
I guess, though, that as they watch me now,
their muscles must burn with vicarious speed.
But this is my race, my impossibility.
I want to break the world record
for slowness, to be by a long shot
the last one there, to wish this bicycle
a quarter inch off the ground so that together
we become a single stationary beast
under which the earth turns leisurely,
bringing the finish line beneath me as I hang
motionless, suspended through nebulae of gnats
and subtle barometric changes,
as close as I can come
to that passion where there is no difference
between the willed absence of motion
and the still absolute of speed.
I want to force myself to admit for once
that this is the only way my life arrives,
wave after wave, breaking on my head, entering
through the five portals of the senses to become
the self, as that man discovered
who slit the retina from a rabbit's eye,
developing the frail tissue to find
the image of his study window,
every arch and space and bar—
the rabbit's last sight transformed
into rabbit itself, into particular rabbit,
imprinted by the weight of light.
See, the crowd approaches me in a torrent!
Oh, that there is anything in this world,
and that it should pass through me in such a way!

Retroactive Causation

This Christmas my mother mailed me an old newspaper
smuggled across the border of disbelief that separates me
from that fabled land, my prehistory

where Floyd Patterson is "ice in a glass,"
and Eisenhower is intricately wrought, as implausible

as Christ's nativity:
God riffling through the calendar,
putting his finger down on the wrong square,
missing me. How could anything happen
before "me"?

Distant and scaled-down, my mother,
wearing the white hat her mother made her buy,
stands beside my father speaking her vows,

tosses the hat into a trash can,
married now, free.

Becoming

I've memorized the life clock at the museum—
nothing but bacteria until a quarter of;
then jellyfish, those bulbous inverse stomachs, God's first try;
reptiles and amphibians flapping and shedding scales;
dinosaurs giving way to the upright ape, and finally,
naked, astonished, shaggily straddling the hour,
the single figure gazing around, unsure of the rules.

What makes sperm whip upstream as if they want something,
navigating dark folds and convolutions,
squirming head to head through steep passageways,
dropping back, scalded in caustic secretions,
snared by ridge or furrow, tails lashing violently
to no purpose, those futures?

The single connection is as specific as any death—
the tubular curved heart forming from outside in,
vertebrae, lung buds, vestigial tail,
bone to fingerprint the hands reaching
to close on clear fluid as nothing takes on density
and the child turns, head down, its first breath
lying in wait on the other side
of the decision the body makes
early or late, the one right time.

This is the voluntary I praise,
the hand that closes around a glass, then lifts it,
the feet that move in one direction and not another,
the flick of the wrist as a letter is mailed or discarded—
all motion that transfers heat
from the ghost realm of the possible
to the textured world of measurement
where intention remains the seed of consequence
as if the world is like the museum's carved egg
that shelters a wooden mica-coated chicken
glistening and guarding in its belly
a stubborn inheritance of eggs.

Greek Myths

Matter was new. It had not finished setting.
Like a cake baked in an overheated oven,
it was soft in the center, and a little runny.
On each page, someone is transformed in a hurry.
The lucky ones have time for farewell speeches.
Fleeing virgins sprout branches, twigs, buds
that instantly flower, as in a time-lapse sequence,
while everybody watches, and the gods,
thwarted again, sit back on furry haunches,
and slyly look around for fleshier victims.
Was it a good time to be alive?
No one knew to ask this sort of question.
They feasted, battled, loved wildly, sacrificed,
bore infants that they cast upon the sea
in wicker baskets, after dire prophecies
that rebounded on them, though they were last to know.
The gods strolled through the landscape in disguise,
as if in boredom or innocent surprise,
not certain yet exactly who they were,
testing their sense of self against the mortals,
and often as not, some casual onlooker
would end up as constellation or as spider;
thus the hard sciences began. How terrifying
for the gods, those nightmare children
loosing their passions as if from live volcanoes,
and each bad wish and bad word coming true!
Indeed, it might be safer to be a star.
Still, the whole place had a small-town feeling.
Everyone knew what everyone else was doing.
Even in Hades they somehow caught the news
and amplified it until it became the future.
There in the mist they intoned it to one another
as if it had already happened, each incident
embellished affectionately in the underworld blues.

Berries

Back then people died often, not bored.
You were playing by the river,
something not yet music tickling your throat,
when you saw the berries, heavy and clustered.
You climbed the hill to bring some to your grandmother.
She crushed one and rubbed it on her lips.
By sundown there was no numbness or blister.
She swallowed a fistful while everybody watched.
The next day when she woke up as always,
you all went down to the river with baskets.

Refuge

It started with punishment—
me with my snarled hair and knotted heart,
tears a dirt paste across my cheeks
as I ran to the apple tree.

Every branch a foothold,
each crook a bony arm to receive me.

I slept there,
silk-rocked in fragrance,
dreaming of nothing,

until the sky lurched sideways
and I woke
falling.

She standing beneath me on the ground.
Over her white skin, hundreds of bees
a gown made of music, a carpet of crawling motion,
each downy body ripe as plush fruit,
ropes of bees clinging to her hair,
halos of bees spinning round her head,
how many of me refracted in all those eyes?

That instant I saw her where she stood
shaking the tree.

The Frog Princess

I used to think she lived at the swimming pool.
Each June at first opening she'd be there
in her lane already, gliding between the ropes
with their red marker buoys, old as she was
with her sloping shoulders and plastic-goggled eyes
and her white legs with humped congestions of veins,
as if she'd wintered there in some outbuilding
behind the maintenance shed or beyond the snack bar,
living on Jujubes and Almond Joy,
amphibious like a frog in her slick brownness,
breaking each morning's ice with her flawless dive,
her brown-skirted swimsuit billowing out
as she flickered at the bottom of the pool
where our lost pennies were, our rings, our earplugs;
while all around the neighborhood in warm houses
Christmas simmered, fragrant in potpourris.
But she's ill, my mother explained one summer.
Her legs hurt her when she isn't swimming.
Her doctor said she'll always be that way.
At the end of the day I'd see her webby flippers
outside her shower stall, and the steam rising
from behind the curtain as she suffered transformation
to mortal woman, limb by rubber limb.

If Worst Came to Worst

In the neighborhood it was always six p.m.
The fathers were always coming home
hatted, briefcased,
stepping out of their cars
like astronauts back from unimaginable orbits,
hailing each other the way fathers knew
in that receding way, like shaking hands without touching
and other tricks that grown men had.
Each key fit its separate slot.
Each door let out its identical wedge of light.
Then the street was empty again,
soaking up the dark.

In the house, patterns of attention reversed themselves
like weather systems on the evening news.
My sister and I released our mother,
who floated toward our father
with his martini.
Ice cubes clinked together
like tiny chimes.
Draw the curtains, girls, she said,
and peering out,
I saw curtains closing in the house next door.

That night his coat hung streaming,
hooked over the top of the closet door.
He spoke of roads closed, bridges out,
shaking his head with a seriousness
approaching pleasure.
We ate supper with the news on,
the voice admonishing travelers,
the room radiant with television luster.
After a while the rain stopped,
but not the wind. Inside that howling
we watched and watched the screen
until with a snap it went hot white

then blank. The air sizzled
into silence. Outdoors, people were standing
on their porches. Stretched across the street
two wires lay crossed and humming.
And up and down the block the fathers warned
until we knew by heart the penalty:
your body stiff as a dog's hit by a car,
your tongue soldered to the roof of your mouth,
your eyeballs going black around the pupils
and no one moving to save you
because even your shoes would be
contagious with light.

And that was when I knew it must have happened
someplace where worst came to worst—
that fated child, another me,
hair jolted out straight, limbs jerking stiff;
and melded onto my jacket, a neighbor
with another neighbor fused to him
hand to shoulder to hand,
just as with the goose of the golden egg;
everyone locked into that single fire,
touching and scorching all the way down the block.

Vampire Tale

Now I can name what then I simply relished
like mints: the taste of torment on her mind.
I saw it was her first time on the school bus.
Having no margins, she begged to be defined,
so I squeezed next to her and told a story
to etch my shadow in her noonday eyes.
She listened in her throat, her skin, her pulse beat—
I was eight years old; she thought me wise.
Even your dad or mama could become one
and suck your blood while you're asleep in bed.
I watched her down the steep steps to the sidewalk.
Her mother waited in a haze of red.

Pyrite

Captain John Smith kneels in the skiff's narrow prow
stabbing the cloudy water with his sword
because in this Virginia of the drowned valleys
a man can reach down to stroke a drumfish six feet long,
or swim with porpoises, or ride in dreams
on great glossy turtles as far as the Antipodes.

This morning on the banks of the Potomac
where a pale precise city will someday grow,
they packed the boat with sand whose gold cast
made them hard and glad, as if they could swallow it,
lining their bellies with the future,
hearts pumping tiny glittering filaments
until each vein gave off light.

Captain John Smith leans out and sends his blade
straight into a shape like a face shifting in the murk,
then reels back, shouting,
the flat-finned stingray writhing on sword point,
the sawtooth spine deep in his wrist.

They prop him in the yellow sand,
watch his arm convulse and swell,
cut his shirt away while the darkness
thickens around him until he cannot tell
if his eyes are open or shut.

But it is that old tease sleep.
At moonrise he sits up,
craving the meat of his attacker,
which he roasts and cuts and eats
all by himself, to the last ounce of flesh.

Flash Bulletin

You know the story
my older sister told me
as she ironed her hair in our room—
Morticia Adams with a halo of steam—
and I on my stomach,
fingering the small white tufts of the bedspread,
overshadowed by the shelf of our mother's dolls
whose teeth were ivory scallops,
whose hair was human hair
whipped and varnished into piled labyrinths,
whose fingernails blazed ten red beams.
The girl and her date in his parked car in the woods.
The escaped murderer with the hook-hand
delivered to them over the radio waves
through the public electricity of the imagination
with his cold steel question.
The white upturning dogwoods releasing their scent.
Kiss, slap, and the inevitable engine sound
grating against that darkness to take them
all the way home
where they find in her door handle
(perfect!) the bloody hook.
My endless wait for everything to begin!
Within me, my cougar's heart
pumped to the rhythm of the possible world.

Jamestown: Anne Burras

My mistress was all wife, innocuous and fair.
On ship she vomited and prayed for grace.
I found my balance when I learned to swear—
silently, in keeping with my station.
She brought two tame doves in a cage of brass,
kissed their sleek necks, and blushed at the sensation
of the soft rush of feathers through her lace,
and when the sailors cooked them, hid her face.

These fierce snows give off an austere blue light
that creeps through chinks in wattle-and-daub walls
to ripple John's bed watery and bright.
I think there is no reason for our luck.
While others pass our door on wooden palls,
we sprout sleep like fur, limb on limb slick
with sweet grease from the bones we suck.

Trying

That time my distant cousin came and went
like someone's fairy godmother, leaving me
The Young Person's Treasury,
a leather-bound book, heavier
than books are supposed to be.
This is what children like you
used to read, my mother said, meaning
this is educational; be appreciative—
but they were not
like me. From the cover
they stared at my sunburned face
and striped Health-tex acrylics.
The girl's hair curled
intricately down her back. Her hands
were folded. She wore
something called a pinafore.
What's a pina for? I giggled
against her silence.
The boy was small, and wore a cap.
They looked older
than was right.
They did not seem to stand
or move the way children do,
yet they were children,
and children read about them,
growing up in their strange clothes
twelve ways, as in the Wonder Bread commercials,
then shrinking again, becoming waxen
and set, reigning from deep velvet chairs
until they died.
This happened a long time ago
before I opened the book.

The first pages were excerpts from the diary
of a girl named Margaret, who was real,
who every evening faithfully recorded

her faults and errors of the day,
her obstinacies and vows of self-improvement.
A quarrel with her brother
over the last drops of cream in the jug.
A disrespectful thought—thought!—
about her mother. *But of my small triumphs,*
she wrote, *I will not speak,*
as I am already inclined to pride.
Was this required?
Did someone check her work,
or did she believe in it, frowning
over the inconveniently bottled ink?
Should I feel sorry for her?
I must take more care
to discipline my will, she wrote
sincerely or not,

and lying on the bed, I wondered
about will. It was not something
we talked about.
There were New Year's resolutions,
but they stayed in quotation marks
that short time until they were
not broken, just forgotten.
My brother and I were neither
good nor bad. We were the ones
we took for granted. My thoughts
remained themselves only, self-regulating
as bees in a hive. Did my mother
monitor her mind like Margaret?
Was will something adult, my bodily fate,
inevitable as breasts?
How far back behind themselves
could thoughts go—
trying to try,
at what place did it stop?

But later, having left the book
in the dimness of my room,
I knew it was all right. My mother
kept no diaries. At night

she watched TV.
Drying dishes, I'd hear the music,
the known laughter. My friends' parents
watched TV, too; the nation did,
both Eastern and Central times—
the images, the life
flowing from the watchers,
one power, one will.
I did not have to make friends with Margaret.
I could hardly make myself believe in her,
so I swallowed her
whole, memorizing her
as she sat there with her journal.
She had lived, she had been
my age once, and living now,
I thought I owed her that.

Pocahontas' Crossing

At sea she learns diamonds: white silk on white linen,
the needle cool and weightless as a splinter from a shaft of light,
thread taut from center, bordered by braid stitch,
thirty-six strokes. Her mind grows dizzy counting so high
with only the good corners to turn her
back and back again, safe between seed pearl and sequin.

On deck her body holds ocean and sky apart, powerful
as that slit of nothing, the needle's eye.
The perfect flatness around her is, they say,
deceptive, like the sense of speed through water.
Even the charts are flat, drawn wrong carefully by men,
then translated into the endless curve
they tell her to take on faith.

In Whitehall she is enclosed by reel and round,
swing and change. Each face is masked.
Double forward, single back,
Sir Roger de Coverly, Pepper is Black,
until the room turns, one compass rose ablaze
with the heat of choosing the right place every time.
Dead reckoning is what she knows
on this sphere whose every point is needle sharp,
the world's end; she dances to keep from falling.

In the Icicle Garden

I harvest the icicles that grow wild from neighbors' eaves.
It's theft, I know, to sever from their glossy roots
these shards of frozen motion for transfer to my lawn,
but my conscience hibernates in winter
like the small and scraggly beast it is.
No mulch, no mites, no maintenance,
only some thirty clear stalagmites in the snow—
witch's garden, shrinkable Stonehenge,
tribute to the hemisphere's estrangement from the sun.
Any one of these could kill a man, I think,
but to plot murder you need charged fingers
and summer blood. Frozen-haired, stiff-coated,
I stand in the center, eavesdropping without a qualm
on the formal meditations of icicles waiting to melt.

Initiation

You were two weeks old.
I'd had half a glass of wine and was feeling
almost normal, bleeding
only a little.
The snow was light
and not unsafe. The steering
was tight. The low beams
parted the darkness
as always with their familiar arc.
Inside the glowing supermarket world
I made choice after choice, with you
strapped to my chest as if I'd plucked you
ripe and wrinkled off some shelf,
so exactly had I charted you
into being twelve hours postovulation
as the books said.
When you are older
I will cut a piece of string
and explain to you how time works,
how we inch along its distance
as ants would, our motion
defined by form.
But that night for no reason
the string was pinched together
in the middle. I paid
for my food. Without interval
I found myself standing in my driveway,
my wallet gone, the groceries gone,
blood streaking my forehead
where I'd cut it leaning into the car door
I was slamming against your foot.
In the house, the telephone was ringing.
Someone had found my wallet
intact. *It was the wine*,
your father said.
It was the effort,

our doctor said. But
if they had filmed that hour
they would have seen me steering my cart
competently through automatic doors,
then stepping down from the curb
to disappear.

On that film, the grocery boy waits
for someone to claim the cart.
My wallet lies by the curb
collecting snow.

Molting

(from a Banks Island legend)

It used to be, people molted once a year.
They didn't even know that it was beautiful.
First the shallow slits on the soles of the feet.
Then the peeling upward with careful hands
over the double knobs of the ankle bone,
along the stretch of calf, knee-rise, thigh-swell,
up and up, the skin slipping off translucent,
the face intact and still, just slightly dry,
then hung on some low tree branch for the wind to stir,
for the large birds to take into themselves
and bring to flight. The new skin smelled like nutmeg
and tingled faintly, and was moist. Old scar tissue,
cuts, burns, wrinkles, bruises and fatigue,
and all remorse lined the intestines of vultures
and powered their swooping. This was instead of death.
Instead of stories. Instead of thousands of tiny pieces
of skin flaking each hour and fluttering off.
And there is no serpent in this version.
There is no apple. There is only an infant,
shriveled as infants have always been, and wailing
at the unfamiliar faces of her parents,
fresh-molted, newly come from the river.
This is where compassion in its haste
does not know it chooses. The mother and father
run to the molting-tree. With their bare hands
they beat off the vultures and retrieve their skins,
which fit quite well, and are ripped only in places.
From now on, there will be no more molting.
See them returning and lifting up their child.
See how the infant quiets in their arms.

Morning Tactics

It's a trick of balance,
of not letting your weight down
on any one thought, of not allying yourself
with either day or night, so for a short while

like Jesus jaywalking across the currents,
like the graceful, leggy insects whose feet
make pinpricks in the water's skin

you are upheld by shifting tides:
your sleep and waking spread beneath you gifts
of buoyancy and flow, until a moment snags you,
and you go under, lost again in floods of light.

Salvation

Who believes in the body
mythologized in books with the colored
cutaway pictures, each section meticulously drawn
on onionskin transparent films,
everything exposed and labeled,
geographical doctrine—the body as Canada,
neighborly, foreign?

This late, the task must be to praise,
omitting nothing, not even the eyelid,
brief journey, miniature portable almost weightless
night without which you would become
the world. Birth's first mercy, it splits
each minute into separate frames for the brain
to splice as if there were no intervals
where what you see disappears, or maybe
you do, and never even know,
just as every detail inside your house
is the same at the end of each day
when you return, with no adjustments to prove
you were ever gone. *Involuntary*
means the body saves you
over and over by a little fold of skin
from all the approaching faces on your street,
each a sun you could fall into.

Map

There's no precision like that of outsider love
where every distance must be drawn to scale
and an inch off means someone absent.

Here is the river together with its name,
water distilled like knowledge
from loss no one remembers.
Here are ink hairs of roads
lashing down the towns, binding the land
against its own unraveling;

legend, landmark,
facts so flat that entropy can't get in;
choices someone made about exclusion;

heartline, lifeline, railroad, bridge,
grid of the defenseless present that consoles
like a night-light or the ending of some story
where word and event become a single place.

Gloucester Women

At dawn Gloucester empties of its men.
Car by car they creep across the bridge
that spans the York River, that murky god
wallowing in its own history, hiding the forgotten glint
of small change, and the bleached and bloated limbs
of drowned watermen. To the Shipyard.
The Naval Base. The Weapons Station.
But at Tina's house the children are arriving—
eight dollars per child per day, the Count Chocula breakfast,
everyone turned outside to play
in Precambrian cars sprouting jagged from the mole-soft ground
like some giant's cracked dentures,
windshields gone now, sides stove in,
and the children steering hell-bent through the galaxy
in their sagging Pampers or cut-off shorts,
barefoot, sunburned, shooting wide laser swathes and shrieking,
I did too get you, dickhead, got you double,
got you infinity, in peril of cuts and falls,
puncture wounds, lockjaw, their own violent
elemental joy. At the window Tina's face
floats in shadows like a small pale balloon.
And next door among her guardian crystals
Carla sleeps thick and dreamless after hours of astral projection
alone in her bed, the bodiless flight through manicured graveyards
and darkened discount stores, across fog-blurred borders,
through rooms of strangers with their foreign quarrels,
over the slow curve of the earth seeking nothing,
everything but her Coast Guard man how many time zones away
not thinking of her. And next door to her Wanda also sleeps
after a night of delivering cartons of Pall Malls, then slipping in
through the tunnel of her driveway beneath vines and trees,
between the bushes that grow wild to shield her
from white people's eyes on this white people's street,
a black Briar Rose in her fortress of brambles
with no kiss coming. Someone should try to paint
these women, lovely and blunt as glass,

with the reflected light that is half shadow,
the brilliance that comes from the careful use of darks
on the Big Island women with their dyed black hair
and their dying coded speech, cousin and cousin
so interbred they are almost one person alone
with the weather, waiting for the scrape of their men's boats;
the Peninsula woman sitting with her youngest son in the red truck
waiting for the school bus at the half-hidden open end
of the unnamed unpaved road two miles from her trailer,
waiting to go home and resist or not
the sacrament of solitude, slug of beer or slice of cake,
who will this day and every day hear only the sounds
that she herself will make;
the woman with the long fat braids and the soft teeth
counting out her coupons at the grocery store one by one,
wasting nothing because she is the strength
for which like the embryo twisting in a love knot under her heart
she is responsible.

Slugs

In Wisconsin every point was hoop-center
beneath the unfurled sky.
We were light there where wind
drilled wood and skin,
and all the houses were shocked
clean by cold.

Here there is a heaviness of waters.
The pines lean in,
giving nothing away.
Even in December the slugs
arrive at dusk on the dining-room wall
as if this house is the first stop
on some slug odyssey.
They could be pieces of intestine, or clear
ribbons of mucus humping across the floor.
Their trails flake into glossy maps
for vacuuming.
There are no basements here.
The underworld runs smack
against my floor—a subterranean garden
of gastropods coiled moistly
round each other, sucking their tiny drinks
of the same groundwater that flows
through well and faucet, tinged with grey sand,
tasting of sulfur.

In Wisconsin everything strained
against lift.
Here all things sink.
The house is losing ground,
the walls shortening perceptibly
month by month,
as the newspaper warns of geologic time,
"transgressions, regressions,"

---

a persistent coastal fickleness.
These slugs are too much older than myself.
I say I do not salt them
because I know I could.

Reliable

Outside their trailers
in dense evening light
the fed men gather to jack and block
their cars' known bodies.
They speak a strict truth
of shaft and strut, choke and bolt,
coaxing out the first obedient spark
that leaps night after night at a piston's stroke
and has nothing to do with going anywhere.

Gravity

A baby fell out of a second-story window
across the street.

Right before that, my husband
is bursting into the room
where my neighbor Joan
sleeps face down on the couch
while the baby clings to the sill outside.

Before that,
my neighbor Sue is forcing her way
through the tick-filled, waist-high grass,
stumbling over decapitated dolls
and wheel-less plastic trucks
to catch the baby as it drops, wailing,
from the bliss of flinging toy after toy to the ground,

and lands against Sue's arm
where the bruise of its fall
stayed for a month.

Before that,
my husband is pounding up the stairs
through the hallways of that fetid house,
calling to anyone who might be home,
reaching out through the low unscreened window
to close his hands
on nothing.

Before that,
my neighbor Amy sees the child hanging,
walks backward into her house
and shuts the door.

Before that,
my husband is not running

---

but somehow hurling himself
across the street.

Before that,
we are finishing lunch,
and get up to check
on some commotion outside.

It starts again
every time I think it,
events streaming like rays of light
from that still point,
the child,
naked except for its diaper,
white against the brown wood of the wall.

We have known since we moved in
that we would not be here long,
that we would in a year or two
leave for a place with trash pickup,
central heat, and street names.
So though I struggled against my indifference
from the first day,
the neighborhood was to me
all memory.

I swept my floors
in circles, from the outside in.
Lit the wood stove.
Went to the monthly parties
for Princess Crystalware
and Undercoverwear Lingerie
and Tupperware,
until there was only
one party, one room
packed with women who have lived here
forever,
whose hairstyles metamorphose regularly,
who with their morning coffee huddle together
to break up their children's fights,
who speak of their husbands with that cynicism

———

that is their special power,
who watch the street,
watch each other,
watch me
with an attention to detail
that is formal, almost sufficient.
They are fierce and kind.
They love quarrels.
At Halloween they paint each other's fingernails
black, with glowing crescent moons.
I come and go in my little car
to the library, to my classes in the city,
and at last to a distant town
to choose a new home.

Then I float down the street
to say good-bye to Sue.
On her arm, the bruise is turning yellow.
She had to kick Joan
three times to wake her,
that sleepy face a map of innocence,
of sofa creases.

I bear Sue's kiss
as I follow the moving van out,
ready again to make up my life from scratch.

What Gifts They Have for Us

The house of dreams is split-level—
rooms within rooms,
stairs like an Escher riddle.
From a higher floor
I am telling my good dead mother
how I know her now that I live her life,
when up the steps two at a time she comes
to clamp a clean diaper
over my nose and mouth,
one lost hand on either side of my face,
stronger than I remember.

Hunger

or

How the Fish Got His Gills

(from a South Pacific legend)

Before you were born.
Before your mother was born.
Before your uncles were born.
When fish could slither on the land.
Three young men wanted me for a wife.
Three young men, and one old fish, a grouper.
Day after day with his thick voice he begged me.
I told him no. He said he could not leave me.
One morning, I saw that he was gone.
I sat on the beach with my red-and-gold cloth, working.
I did not look toward the other side of the inlet.
Sly over the white sand, silent behind me,
slap into the water I was tumbled
all the way down his throat, if fish have throats.

And how I drove him then, that startled lover,
with what speed, what awful undulations,
steering the spindly curve of his white bones,
peering out through his glassy eyes to see
the whole ocean bulging and fixed before me,
his moist thoughts lining the inside of my mouth
like unborn pearls, or little eggs to suck,
I his false heart, the load of his desire,
and *o-o-o!* was all that he could say
until I tired, and with my sewing shell
I slit him up both sides, and out I swam
through that bloody sluice, my hair an ink cloud
around the roughness of his scaly face.
My people hymned as a goddess then
with oils, corals, garlands, and perfumes.
And from that moment on he only breathed
through his wounds, as lovers always do.

Psyche and Her Sisters

The story has it wrong. It is not the god
they speak of, but themselves, their lives.
Behind the wall he crouches, wings bunched small
and tight. Their talk is women's talk—
spiraling, unsimple. Night after night
is this what Psyche wants, burrowing
into his chest, crying *tell*?
There are brides who would invade
the fleshy chambers of your heart
to grasp the secret patterned snake
that is your life, unwind it
coil by coil so they could say
I know you. He shivers in no shadow.
For god or man to take a wife
is to risk womanspeech,
the lamp and knife.

Telling the Truth

On the late news the five teenagers pray in Yugoslavian
in a single voice, lambent and sure,
until with sudden gravity they drop to their knees
as the Virgin appears to them but not in the camera.
I see her as clearly as I see you, one had said
in the interview portion chosen from all the footage
along with the shots of a woman's rosary
transformed from pearl to gold
as the tour bus approached the mountain village.
Will it change back again, or is faith a border
that color cannot cross?

I have known such faces, the dilating pupils,
the slight flare of nostrils,
the lips moving rapidly with mysteries.
In high school we used to fall backward in slow motion,
crumpling to the ground with holy cotton bones
as the visions struck, and the worst thing now
would be to say that it did not happen, all of it,
even though the heat is dissipated,
the angels gone. We had no language,
no persecution, no Yugoslavian grandmothers
to filter the short rays of God
that seared the egg-white mucus of the conjunctiva,
lining our eyeballs with cloud.
Our prayers have become cautious and correct.
I lean forward into the screen
to see if any of them blink.

Marvels

l times and in all places
ugh luck or work or thievery, someone
tting what they need.
They are astonished, and take it
personally. At this moment everywhere
for no reason someone's particular hope
is now dismembered before their eyes.
They too are astonished, and take it
personally. The good child prays
Thy Will Be Done, but the world's voice
rasps raw and inappropriate its *want, want*
while time grows thick as music
from rude desire of leaf and cell.
In Rublev's icon of the Trinity,
Sarah gazes unseen from her barren house
whose root is the Father's head.
Wings, haloes, hands
frame the lamb Isaac,
who floats fetus-curled and ready,
a small intrusion in the golden cup.

Claims Adjustment

How to stop defining myself
by what nearly happened,
quit testing the body-sized gap
between the first sparks and the last backwash of flame,
as if memory is faulty as the car's transmission?

For the senses, time is not abstract.
They know the intimacy of chance,
the presence of the self in that almost place
where I ignite, a witch or martyr
in private apocalypse behind smoke-sealed windows.

I believe in combustion.
I have faith in cause and effect.
But by what formula do I exorcise loss
that always recedes into its negation?
With what speech do I make countercharm
against transformation that did not occur?

I'll say it was just postponement—
when I take inventory, count myself
with everything that did not burn.

The Nursery-Web Spider

It has been snowing without pause for two days.
For the last hour she has been catching spiders,
to take outside to the woodpile—
lifting them one by one in the slick blue world-bowl,
the curved sides sudden and sheer around them,
tilt and swirl, silent feet on china,
gripless. In the tiny black bead of arthropod memory,
in the ink pool of ancestral consciousness,
there is no knowledge that could have prepared them for this
swift rapture of the heights, the spider bends,
air-pressure cramp and no breath left
to craft the architecture of escape.

Now she has offered her colored spools to her children
and curled up on the living-room couch to take a nap.
The children have her fine features,
thin hands, pale fairy-godmother hair.
She is, in fact, dreaming of lost long hair,
its weight and constant presence against her skin,
inconvenient, mysterious.
What can I do for you? the stylist had asked her
when she sat down in the plastic-covered chair,
believing the open-endedness of that offer.
In her dream now she is like her daughter's doll
whose hair you can pull from an opening in her head
farther and farther until it reaches her toes,
as if her body is hollow, stuffed with hair.

Sink and surface, wake and drift again.
The children have tired of cat's cradle
and are looping the thread around chair back and table leg,
lamp pole, and over the top of the couch,
silver, crimson, black, gold,
and she sees their innermost parts, the tiny glands
that spin out thread like liquid silk—
dragline, bridge, drop and backtrack,

center hub, spiral and web frame.
The spider's mouth is toothless, small,
designed for sucking, she'd read aloud.
It wraps up its breathing food like a shining mummy.
But where does the book name
the delights of balance, the self-intimacy of hanging
windwise from invisibly trembling strands?
Blessed are egg sacs, for they contain
numerous ticklish possibilities.
In the woodpile the spiders have pinpoint human faces.
Snow seals the windows, emitting radiance.
The children are nesting in her yard-length hair.
The nursery-web spider's home is strung with light.

Cost

Even Dante, though he saw the girl just twice,
in the unambiguous light of memory
looked at her for the first time
again and again, startling himself
every day throughout the rest of his life
because he knew that first times count
only in retrospect and in conclusion.
Therefore, choose what you love over and over,
recalling it while you spit the toothpaste out
or close your eyes to wander into sleep.
Strengthen the neural pathways that lead to it.
In your own dark it shines privately for you,
whatever it is, vengeance or safe delight.
But remember Dante's dream: the cloud of unfurled fire
surrounding the terrible god who holds in his palm
a flaming heart—*Vide cor tuum*—and in the god's arms
sleeping, the naked Beatrice, whom he wakens,
to feed her that living heart whole until she weeps.

Explicit

Suppose I could do it,
suppose I could go back there—
if *there* is the name of that place
where I used to live—
to that room where my younger self is sleeping,

and whisper her awake
to offer her my current version
of a long-range traveler's advisory,
trusting her memory, her interpretations,
watching her judge me
from underneath the sheets where she lies
in the blue sprigged nightgown I'd forgotten—
knowing that I could touch her hand,
a stranger's hand, since I would be the ghost;
and that if I went to the window
the night on the other side of the screen
would seem no less cryptic for having been
lived through both forward and in reverse;
and beyond the bedroom door I could hear
my parents laughing at "Get Smart,"
which used to be funny.

Resist me, child!
Call for help,
the slit of light slashing the dark
as the door opens,
as our mother, alive and in a hurry,
comes to banish the ghoul, the child molester
of the pasty face and appropriate stories.

Loss of Advantage

It is the greenhouse effect that saves us.

Through the thick glass of the Outerwear Museum
children view wool and mohair,
then run home to bad dreams of L. L. Bean coats
pursuing with empty arms.

One noon under relentless television lights
the President sends his tie flying,
unbuttons his shirt and strips it off,
peels away the wet white undershirt,
steps out of his pants, a statue rising out of stone
while cameras whirr like cicadas in the glare
and members of the press do the respectful thing
until the floor is piled high
with pressed and pleated linen and silk.

Before long, naked soldiers drill
as if to cartoon music,
then quit, embarrassed.
Words soften and slow, no longer packed hard enough
to bore their way toward heart
through layers of fabric, that oblique distance.
Now every other is just like you—
flesh and fur and the capacity for pain,
seeing the map of your own death
etched in blue across your neighbor's throat,
measuring the gap between the ribs
where the knife could slip,
your skin knowing that slit
would fit you perfectly.

Fifth Brandenburg

Here mathematics has become prayer,
testing the pulse of time.

Here change and counterchange accumulate
until there is nothing left over

while expectation overcomes gravity,
resolving into the final key.

The violin speaks in tongues
and the flute interprets.

The harpsichord qualifies metamorphosis,
praising that which is fixed.

The principle of silence is accuracy.
The purpose of meter is ascent

through the narrow lattice of sound and will
where the human gift is to make distinctions.

All Souls

The skeleton, the wolf, and the mummy
have dragged me into the darkened chapel
so they can eat their candy in delicious fear.
Tonight I went out as a mother
because I know how to make good talk,
to watch for hidden roots
and stumps buried in leaves.
But hard in my belly is the pomegranate seed.
If my living will can ebb so slow and chilled,
I wonder who it is believers speak to
when they invoke the dead alphabetically in chant
as if they could step down from the windows
and all the bats fly free
through their spaces in the glass?
Their names are abandoned
like dry locust shells,
flesh and bone dissolved
into our bodies
that are their relics.

Inside the closed jewel box of the sanctuary
my companions name their candy
by touch and scent in whispers.
The wolf demands from me a story.
Then follow me, I say.
Here in this locked box is Bishop Cole's chalice.
On his deathbed he begged to be buried with it,
but the Church refused.
And I tell them of the photograph in which, dead,
he appears standing behind it, surfacing wetly
through the pan of fixer in someone's darkroom
as if through inverse baptism.
Could he be here now? they ask,
touching the box just barely,
glad when I assure them
that he could.

And in this creaking chapel
I honor him for his unrepentant love
of silver, the sheen and form and heft
of a single object he couldn't leave behind,
having become his own desire.
For the first time in months
I can feel my own body,
specific and distinct,
joint and limb and heartbeat
where there is yes to the skeleton,
yes to the mummy and wolf,
to the vital tension of tiredness held in time,
to the saints in their windows,
particular, awake,
to the morning's lifted cup
in which everything
is willed—this darkness,
all doctrines of transformation.

That

Deep now in the thicket of family,
I cautiously honor
that which causes trouble,
each *no*, all fluctuation
and stubbornness.

Alive.
Hidden under reasons, camouflaged
as reason, just as certain
reptiles flicker and vanish against tree trunk
or forest floor. Stipple-backed,
fluid, older than us and not
necessarily warm-blooded.

The way it passes in and out between us.
The story goes, a wet nurse saw it once
slipping into the cradle, tail disappearing
through the sleeping child's mouth,
and wise, she did nothing to hinder
that holiness.

Like the salamander, it writhes
in flames, lies still as you approach.
You reach to grasp the corpse,
and in a clump of ash you see
winking, one ruby eye.

To My Son, Who Is Afraid of Bugs

For you, butting your heavy head
into my waist, as if to seek return,
I'd fill the house with light.
Let it be something like neon, blue and cool.
Then let the doors swing clear of every hinge,
and razor blades slice open all the screens.
Let the roof fold back like a dollhouse roof
that they may come: beetles like speeding brooches
with their rubber-band-twanging clicks,
their thin-spun false eyelash legs and feet.
And flies—black-goggled, wedding-veil winged,
with their ellipses and backward figure eights,
beaked and hollow-tongued, inky clots of motion.
From eggs in stagnant creek and marshy pond
let the mosquitoes rise, whining perpetual G,
dangling their prehistoric shadows
like nightmares you could bridle and ride off on.
And the moths with their dusting of feathery shingles;
delicate poison-green luna of the counterfeit eyes,
double-winged catocala with its flasher's coat.
Tiny gravity-defying filaments,
furry or striped, with bulging compound vision,
let them all come fluttering in
on waxy wings and pairs of jointed legs,
buzzing and whirring or riding their own silence.
Let them be loved for the staccato dance
the dark makes of their mindless desire for light.
Then let that light expand to burst the bulbs—
let them feast on waves of it as it filters
through abdomen, thorax, antennae, probiscus, mouth parts,
until inside the mosquitoes our blood strobes purple,
and the flies become like little radiant flowers,
and the moths angels, and when they all rest winking
on our hair like glowing flocks of crowns,
and dangle from our ears like pirate jewelry
you may break free from me to laugh and reach
for all the colors our wanting sparks the world.

Technology

Should I feel sorry
for my children as they stand
spellbound in TV World at the mall,
a hundred screens flickering around them,
most with the tiny extra
square in one corner so you can watch
two shows at once?
Approaching from a distance,
I pretended that the room
was on fire. Should I whisk them away
from this conflagration, or is it already
too late, the knowledge of such simultaneity
burning into them as their eyes adjust
to bombardment? I've been warned
that even car travel is bad
for children's vision, that constant
focusing and refocusing at high speeds
weakens the developing eyes. But I am tired
of guilt, tired of believing
that with enough good-mother
willpower I could turn us into the Amish families
we pass sometimes in their buggies,
tired of trying not to be in every way
omnivorous. If there is a human destiny
let us approach it at our different speeds—
the virtuous ones slowing farther and farther down,
the greedy ones like me
accelerating, until we overtake
each other because
everything we love and fear is ours now
and was from the beginning when together
we imagined all of it.

Not Thinking about God

The room is deep in distinct and focused stillness
and this insurance form is not getting done,
which is a kind of self-indulgence,
so I will pick up my pen and make the small serious black marks
because it is almost ten-thirty, and the mail carrier
is driving her truck up the state route toward my house,
and throughout the United States Postal Service
letters are pouring in like so many fish
slapping their tails in great aluminum bins,
and distribution clerks in uniforms are sorting them
zip code by zip code, according to the big blue book.
In Marietta, Georgia, the whole world's baby-sitter
is shuffling in her slippers and crisp new flowered housedress
to her mailbox at the bottom of the driveway,
where she will find the home permanent-wave kit she ordered
with the small-size rods, and the curl solution and the neutralizer
in their separately labeled gold plastic squeeze bottles,
and on her way back to the front door she will be thinking
that when all the children are asleep—
the round retarded one and the one with the oozing eye
and the smart fast one who pulls records out of their jackets,
Crystal Gayle and Kenny Rogers and Willie Nelson
naked and helpless in piles on the living-room carpet—
she will sit at her clean kitchen table
and tape cotton strips all the way around her hairline
to prevent burns. And in New York, New York,
a city so potent it backfires, sounding twice,
in a high-swaying office that might have broken loose
into the glinting sky without anyone even noticing,
the mail is rattling by on a metal cart
and everyone is filling coffee mugs
and shaking out tiny pink fluorescent packets of pretend sugar
and the woman at her desk on her second day there
is holding five letters in her hand and thinking
that someday in a month maybe, or a little longer,
this will all be something she does without noticing,

---

and her whole body will feel safer and more blurred
and not so alert, and how comfortable and a bit sad
that will be in a month or so, or by Christmas, at least;
and everywhere bad news is leaking out of envelopes like radiation,
and good luck is floating in on skinny flat promissory notes,
and the *Reader's Digest* is spreading its old Pelagian gospel,
and the whole country is veined by streets and roads
with little trucks going and coming through the autumn light
from stop to stop, from name to living name.

The Gift: 1578

It is December.
The Queen's tooth ticks
hot through her head.
For two full days and nights she has not slept,
yet bars from her chamber the tooth-drawer Fenatus.
She has an orphan's terror of parting with what's hers,
hard won, as Lady Bryan wrote Lord Cromwell
that when the baby Elizabeth cut her double teeth,
surely she'd stop fretting, and delight the King.

In the garden of Elizabeth's fourteenth year
Catherine Parr's clean white hands held the princess down
while Lord High Admiral Seymour cut
into a hundred pieces her black gown.

On Coronation Day as her foot touched the Abbey's threshold
the throngs outside hurled themselves
upon the purple carpet of her entrance,
and with knife and ragged tooth
ripped it to pieces for remembrance.

In her last winter the jewel cutter
will file off the Coronation Ring
grown into the tissue of her skin.
Elizabeth turns.
Her chamber is filled with men.
Her eyes, ringed like a raccoon's,
seal tight in refusal when they tell her
it is time now for the extraction.

Someone's fingers lace themselves through hers.
She does not lift her head,
but hears John Aylmer, Bishop of London, speak:
See, my few remaining teeth
I offer for your service.

From the white world of her silk bed
through glittering slits of eyes
she watches Fenatus pluck the Bishop's tooth.

The Queen sits up,
opens her mouth like a hungry infant.

John Aylmer bites down hard on his own blood
and briefly knows all times
curved as glass around this instant
where nothing is lost,
not tooth or touch or thought,
and sleep approaches the bed
like a slow swan where the Queen lies back,
a child, healing.

Properties of Salt

(In the Reliquary)

If it were not for the salts,
I could tie knots in these bones.

Memory is the present of things past,
Augustine wrote. I say that salt
is the memory of substance,
recalcitrant as what has been.

Everything organic dissolves,
unable to bear the light,
but salt disciplines history,

femur and phalanx translated into stories
we piece together with hungry hands that know
truth is the work of salt, the gift of bone,
the only reason we name them holy.

Shrinking

The sons of God were giants, and they walked the earth.
Enormous spoor plopped steaming in their tracks
to become cities windowed by the slightest pressure of a thumb,
hardening into glossy clay.
In those days there was neither
subtlety nor melancholy, and the young trees wondered
at the first congestion of heartwood.

If this is legend, it is locked in the cerebral cortex.
Even now, each child is born huge, world-fisted,
to rock in the tidal sea of unconsciousness
like Paul Bunyan in his boat-cradle,
until the first face hovers overhead, a balloon
dipping, grinning, the original differentiation.
With every connection the child shrinks,
and with it, the world.
Crayolas roll across the table,
and color itself is split
and split again—sepia, burnt orange,
Indian gold. From first grade
there is no distance to adult
knowledge of knowledge,
to the awareness even in sleep
of the existence of the twenty-one kinds of knots,
Braille, and the heart of a light bulb
where hairlike filaments burn in silence
suggesting some bright correspondence between things,
creation's manic phase.

You who would drag us back
to the place where stars were not yet old
long-distance information:
Read the *Weekly World News!*
Human spontaneous combustion is epidemic.
Even now, at the local shopping mall
a kissing couple bursts into flames,

though the kiss is only brief
and superficial, as prescribed.
The gaps between events
collapse. Everything
is being named and known,
and with each naming
the world contracts a size
until at the end it will be
a marble of impossible density
shot through with colored veins,
that fits inside the smallest jewel box,
and some local angel will flick the hasp.

Resolution

In the catalogue of the world
let us name a space for wasted motion.
With precision let us remember
the hand washers at their white sinks
scrubbing nothing away;
the nail biters tenderly intimate
with each brittle crescent.
At her mirror the unchosen girl
practices the parade wave over and over,
her arm shaping invisible patterns of heat.
In a densely curtained parlor the thick stepsister
bloodies her foot against the crystal slipper.
In his chamber the alchemist stirs the luminous fluid
forever a change away from transmutation.
Up the driveway in their sober shoes
troops of witnesses are crunching
to save us from that end for which they long
when the hand washers are clean to the bone
and the little crescents shine like infant moons
when the girl's hair fans out brighter than crowns,
the slipper softens and melts to any foot,
the base elements marry one another
and our skins pop and split like pods,
all our lost energy of choice released,
fierce from the first moment we intended.

Distances

I love calling west through time zones,
the telephone company's map open before me
with its miniature clocks and the deep fissure
in the middle where the binding is,
my disembodied voice traveling left
past the sprinkling of familiar cities on the East Coast
through the places where weather is harvested
and states grow bigger, their names
more voweled, where the Green Giant
lies staked to the ground,
the weight of his body flattening the Midwest,
the foliage of his hair ripe for shearing,
for the preserving cold of refrigerated trucks.
I love the fact that there is no discernible
elapsed time between exit and entrance,
that my voice circumnavigates the hidden passages
of someone's ear before I pause for breath.
For that listener it is not yet evening,
though beyond my window the outlines of trees blur
as if the onset of night gives them permission
to loosen the boundaries of their thingness
while my voice journeys back in time
to the afternoon where everyone is always
a few hours behind me, more innocent.
And I could be there too; I could fly westward
shedding seconds along the way, arriving
before I phoned, to answer my own call,
that abstraction, and rush my words
forward along the line, to interrupt myself
at the moment my plane crosses overhead
and I look down through layers of cloud light
to seek the intersection of my voices
where self, released from place, at last consists of
the velocity of union it attains.

UNIVERSITY PRESS OF NEW ENGLAND publishes books under its own imprint and is the publisher for Brandeis University Press, Brown University Press, Clark University Press, University of Connecticut, Dartmouth College, Middlebury College Press, University of New Hampshire, University of Rhode Island, Tufts University, University of Vermont, and Wesleyan University Press.

ABOUT THE AUTHOR   Claire Bateman lives in Clemson, South Carolina. She was the winner of the 1990 Louisiana Literature Poetry Prize and was a finalist that year for both the Walt Whitman Award and the Brittingham Prize. Her work has appeared in such places as *Louisiana Literature*, *Cimarron Review*, and *Cumberland Poetry Review*. In 1991 she was the recipient of an NEA fellowship.

Library of Congress Cataloging-in-Publication Data

Bateman, Claire.
The bicycle slow race / Claire Bateman.
    p.   cm. — (Wesleyan new poets)
ISBN 0-8195-2196-5. — ISBN 0-8195-1198-6 (pbk.)
I. Title.   II. Series.
PS3552.A826884B5   1991
811'.54—dc20   90–28734